Th

G000141114

A TO B GUIDE TO

DEALING WITH DIFFICULT BOSSES

BRIAN GUEST

www.thrive-careers.com

ISBN 978-1-908964-00-7

Thrive Careers Ltd.

www.thrive-careers.com

ABOUT THRIVE

Thrive Careers specializes in providing leading career development information, mentoring and coaching products and services to professionals and corporate clients around the world.

Created to support managers and executives with their career challenges and development objectives, Thrive is at its core a promoter of self-development and effective leadership.

This guidebook series, along with Thrive's other product ranges, are designed to suit the objectives and busy schedules of modern day professionals by providing cost-effective expertise, interactivity and flexibility to clients. For more information on our other guidebooks, self-assessment tools, coaching and mentoring products visit our website:

www.thrive-careers.com

Thrive Careers Ltd. is based in London, United Kingdom.

THRIVE A TO B GUIDEBOOKS

This series is written for managers and executives who wish to develop their core skills and those of their teams.

Each guidebook draws on the practical experience of a top executive coach and senior business leader. This breadth of experience helps you see the bigger picture and provides state-of-the-art thinking and tools for achieving positive and sustainable change.

In this series Thrive aims to support and challenge you in your learning and development with a blend of coaching and mentoring approaches. Not only does this grant you access to top quality resources derived from in-depth experience, but also frames them in a way that you can relate to your own circumstances and challenges.

Executive coaching is one of the most powerful and effective ways for leaders and managers to develop their skills and performance. But working one-to-one with a top coach is not always feasible.

The A to B guides give you access to several of the advantages of coaching in a cost-effective and just-in-time approach. You will be constantly challenged to assess your own situation – where you want to get to and how best to get there. It's all about achieving results effectively, efficiently, economically and sustainably. To do this you will be using tools that top professional coaches use with their clients to help you coach yourself and others. You will also be challenged to find the changes that are going to give you the biggest improvement and given advice on how to tackle diverse situations you may encounter.

The series is designed to be easy to work through and to store most of your key notes and plans so that they become working documents. This aspect, coupled with the common structure and layout, make them easy to refer back to and to sustain your learning and progress.

CONTENTS

GETTING THE MOST OUT OF THIS RESOURCE

- Consider your overall work context and write down your boss's and your major challenges. This will help give context and priorities to the development of your working relationship with your boss.

Your boss's challenges:

_____

_____

_____

_____

Your challenges:

_____

_____

_____

_____

- Review the overall structure first.

- Go through the guidebook in sequence, completing the exercises and self-assessments as set out.

- Get feedback from others as suggested.

- Mark areas you wish to return to think about or understand more fully.

- Highlight areas you believe could be key to your own progress and that resonate strongly with you.

- Follow the guide to producing your own developmental goals using the Challenge-Priority Brainstorming Chart and Thrive Action Plan located in the Appendix of this guidebook. Be positive and get going!

- Create a mentor or thinking partner relationship at work to challenge and support you on your journey: someone who you believe has and deserves a good reputation in the area of your developmental need.

- Consider creating a small focus group to meet periodically and share thoughts on particular challenges and dilemmas any of you are facing in this area of development.

- Incorporate a reread of the guide into your action plan.

THE A TO B METHODOLOGY

The A to B methodology is based upon the premise that we have the ability to change and develop in the ways that we really want to.

There are four key questions:

- Where am I? This is "**A**." This sometimes has an element of being "stuck" about it – think of it as a red stoplight impeding you from continuing your journey.

- Where do I need to get to? This is "**B**." Imagine it as the blue sky you see when you reach the top of a mountain that makes you realize just how much you've achieved throughout your journey.

- What barriers are in my way and how can I overcome them?

- What else do I need "**TO**" get there? Think of this as the green traffic light that has come on to let you progress with your journey.

Where you are is where you are. **A** is **A**. It helps to accept this gracefully. Some things have gone well and perhaps some things could have gone better. We can calmly learn from the past, but we cannot let it keep absorbing us, especially if the emotions it evokes are negative for us. Some unwanted or disliked things might seem present in **A**, they may seem to be out of our control. How we react to them inside ourselves, however, is ultimately under our control.

Imagine holding where you are, represented by a big letter **A**, in the open relaxed palm of your left hand (or right hand if you are left-handed), and where you are going, represented by a big letter **B**, in your other palm, which is raised up a foot higher than the other palm. You need to let go of any strong emotions about **A** and feel excited and positive about improving to **B**.

You have particular strengths and development needs. These can depend on circumstances, both inside yourself – for example, your mood, stress or energy levels – or in your external environment – for example, the pressures in your particular business.

Sometimes we can accurately understand our actual position. Sometimes we need input or feedback from others to see our position more clearly. This often applies to personal relationships with our bosses as there are so many factors and viewpoints involved.

In learning things we often go through the following phases:

- Unconscious incompetence – We don't know that we don't know something important about dealing with our boss.

- Conscious incompetence – We know that we don't know something important in dealing with our boss.

- Conscious competence – We consciously follow a way of working with our boss.

- Unconscious competence – We automatically follow good practices with our boss without having to consciously follow something like a process plan or checklist.

We learn best by leveraging our strengths – our learning preferences and building on our positive experiences and talents. Very often we see the glass as half-empty instead of half-full. A positive attitude is important in making progress.

Next you need to know where you want to get to. This needs to be a better place; better in terms of what you value. It might not be perfect, but it is better and will meet most of your priority needs.

Finally, you need a clear plan for what you need to do to get to that better place. You need to identify the challenges and support or resources you need to grow and develop into the new position.

1. INTRODUCTION TO DEALING WITH DIFFICULT BOSSES

Working life is full of challenges and one of the toughest to get right can be how to deal with the boss. They may be a joy to work for or could be rude, egotistical, indecisive and stubborn. Regardless, learning how to master the boss-employee relationship will impact your career significantly.

There are three main signs that your boss's behavior is dominating your life; physical, mental and emotional. At an extreme physical signs include frequent headaches, chest pains, stiffness, nausea, fatigue and insomnia. Mental signs involve overthinking, revenge fantasies, often staring into nothing or you find it hard to concentrate. The emotional signs manifest themselves as feelings of inadequacy, pressure, anxiety or anger. Though these are all severe symptoms, many abandon their career within an organization largely due to a difficult boss. Wouldn't it be great to learn how to manage this relationship to help you achieve your objectives and make life at work better?

You are likely to have many bosses along your career. Each boss will have his or her own personality, strengths, weaknesses and preferences. They can also have different communication styles, different ways of delegating and dealing with conflict. They may also have a different hierarchy of values and a different corporate, national or regional cultural background.

This guidebook will focus on general boss-relationship issues and provide advice as well as guidance in dealing with 5 key challenging boss personalities. These are the indecisive, self-centered, bullying, unappreciative and control freak bosses.

For many a difficult or bad boss is a constant source of stress and frustration at work. Maybe it's the excessive workload they burden you with or the refusal to listen to any suggestion you may have – we've all experienced situations like these and inevitably will again in the future. Your boss may be a tough nut to crack, but improving the relationship and work dynamic are definitely not impossible. With time, effort and perseverance following the tips this guidebook provides, you should see changes at work you may not think are possible at present.

It's also important to understand our own personality and boss preferences. We may find others get on really well with a boss that we find difficult. After all, a relationship is a two way thing.

Indeed one of the biggest mistakes made in dealing with bosses is the assumption that it is the boss's sole responsibility to manage the relationship. It's natural to make this mistake – "after all he/she is the boss."

2. BENEFITS OF AN IMPROVED BOSS-EMPLOYEE RELATIONSHIP

- Life at work is **more enjoyable**. You are probably no longer asking yourself "why am I doing this?" Instead you are happy to do it; you can feel you are getting somewhere at work and are receiving more recognition and appreciation from your boss. This in turn helps you to be self-confident and enjoy high morale.

- Life at work is **less stressful**. The little things don't get to you as much once you've mastered how to work well with your boss and handle both the regular day-to-day and difficult situations that arise.

- Work is **more productive**. Negative stress and tension can be substituted by positive energy and a more focused attitude. Working well together with your boss can be wonderful for your productivity and getting the support and resources you need to deliver quality results.

- Your newfound ability to manage the relationship with your boss well won't go unnoticed. You'll find you have **more influence** and **greater promotion possibilities** at work. It will also help gain you respect from others in the organization.

- As you learn to understand your boss better you will be **more prepared** to handle new situations and make them work in your favor.

- While you meet the boss's objectives you'll be increasing the chances of **meeting your personal objectives** also – be it a raise, promotion, new role, more control or getting your ideas or pet project accepted. Indeed your boss is more likely to mentor you and help you to see where your talents lie if they warm to you. Your boss can be a useful advisor in helping you see the best career paths for yourself.

- By knowing what it takes to improve a boss-employee relationship and how this improved relationship can benefit the organization, you will **become a better boss and manager yourself**.

- You will learn to become **better at managing conflict and difficult personalities**, a skill to carry with you throughout your working and personal life.

3. "A" – KNOWING YOUR BOSS

It isn't uncommon to hear people say "I can't stand working with my boss." As different as your personalities, work styles and priorities may be, holding negative attitudes towards your relationship with your boss is counter-productive and will only hurt your prospects within an organization. You might like to believe you have all the knowledge and the means to advance within a company, but your future is often decided upon by your boss and other senior personnel. Bosses can have the political influence to help further your career, get the resources you need to perform well and offer you guidance to further success. Your boss got to where he or she is within the organization somehow and there is definitely something you can learn from this regardless of your boss's difficult personality.

3.1   Understanding your boss

The mental image you have of your boss may look like a mouse or Godzilla, but in reality your boss is very much a human. Good managers accept their bosses are prone to human failings and take responsibility for their own career development.

Instead of giving up, the best managers look to understand their boss and themselves better and use this information to seek growth and improvement in their careers.

Understanding your boss begins with knowing your boss's goals, strengths, weaknesses, work style and pressures.

Your boss's goals will be a mix of personal and business goals. Is your boss looking to advance from Regional MD to CEO? What goals does your boss have to deliver? Profit targets, successful merger or perhaps administrative overhaul? Do not make assumptions about your boss's goals as this can be detrimental. If you were to assume your boss is looking to achieve gradual business growth when instead he/she is looking to generate large short term profits to keep his/her job you may be fired for not helping achieve this objective. Generally bosses do pass on their budget figures and targets to those below them but they might not discuss other qualitative goals in as much detail. Discuss with your boss whether the overall objective now is to reduce costs, seek long term growth, brand development or new business and investment etc.

Strengths will range from specific skills to greater capabilities. Does your boss have excellent people skills, persuasive skills, negotiation skills, sales abilities or creativity? Also, is your boss business savvy, a marketing genius, a financial expert, organized or a perfectionist?

Weaknesses, like strengths, will relate to specific skill deficiencies and general areas of weakness. Is your boss bad with finance but outstandingly creative? From your experience does your boss need to improve his/her deal-making skills, presentation skills, political savvy, et cetera?

Work style is all about how your boss likes to work. Does your boss like to be very organized with strict deadlines and scheduled meetings? Is your boss's work style very relaxed? Does your boss prefer written reports or open discussions? What kind of work atmosphere is your boss most comfortable with? How and when does your boss socialize with staff? Does he or she do lunches or play a sport? What does your boss find fun and funny? Is your boss a very private person?

Use this knowledge of your boss's preferred work style to your advantage. If your boss likes to be very productive with his/her time wouldn't it be better to pass on figures and work updates before business meetings so you can start discussing the important business questions right away? If you notice the boss likes to visualize how the business is doing rather than read about it, use visual material in your presentations or suggest a visit to the "shop/factory/branch floor" to see for themselves what you are trying to get through to them. Use what you know and think ahead about how you can work better together with your boss.

Last of all, are there pressures from those around your boss? What sorts of things does your boss's boss demand from him/her? What pressures are there from their direct reports, less senior personnel and peers around the same level as your boss? Bosses can hide some of the pressures they are facing, be these political or personal. Those who have been in the business for longer than you or are closer to the boss than you will probably be more aware of these. It is these people who will be able to "spill the beans," but be subtle in the way you inquire about this. Your objective isn't to dig dirt or gossip, it is to be more aware of your boss's pressures and with this knowledge help improve your relationship and further your career.

Use the 360 degree chart below to write a few keywords that describe your boss.

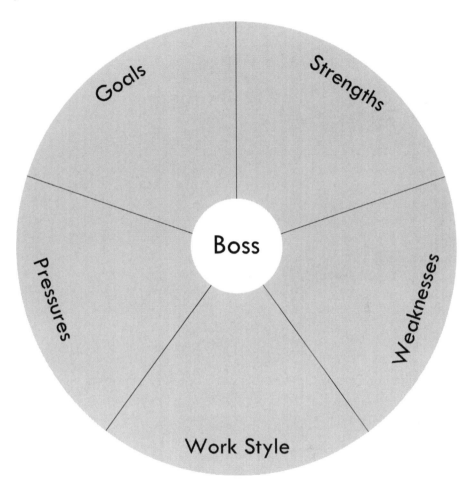

3.2 Difficult boss personality traits

There is no personality description that will fit your boss 100% of the time. People are complex creatures with many facets to their personalities. The five key difficult personality traits discussed in this guidebook should help you better manage tough aspects of your boss's personality. Note that it is possible for a boss who is a bully to also be unappreciative and self-centered. But in order to help you manage your boss better you need to focus on individual aspects of your boss's personality and tackle each one at a time.

Indecisive

Decision-making is a skill your boss may not be good at. If your boss is indecisive he/she will often struggle to make decisions and pick between options when under stress or during a period of crisis. Indecisive bosses can often be quite insecure and have weak leadership skills. Their response to questions and team discussions are often vague and aren't focused on finding solutions. Instead they seem to get lost in details and their own thought processes.

Decisions can have positive and negative outcomes. Good decision-makers will develop their best decision based on the available circumstances and go ahead with it. If things later turn sour they accept their mistake and look to make necessary adjustments or corrections and move on. Indecisive people are caught focusing on the possible negative outcomes of their decisions, this leads them to procrastinate and avoid decision-making altogether. There is always a time, however, when employees need a decision to progress with their work or meet corporate objectives. When the indecisive boss procrastinates, employees quickly become frustrated with the lack of direction and fast-approaching deadlines.

Self-centered

The self-centered boss, as the name would suggest, is all about "me, me, me!" Your boss either has a big ego or is very self-absorbed. These kinds of people care little about other's feelings, morale or objectives. They often think they know-it-all, are assertive and dislike being told they are wrong. A boss with this personality trait can give little time to your ideas and quickly refutes any suggestions you have that he/she judges to be inferior. Sometimes this kind of boss likes to make him/herself look good to their superiors and shareholders without giving others around them much credit for their work.

Bully

The bully likes to feel superior and in control. To do this they push their subordinates into tasks that achieve their personal objectives and sometimes even pointless tasks simply for a sense of superiority. As bullies at school, the bully in the office often forms a clique of like-minded people. Those outside this clique often feel uneasy and threatened by the boss. To the bully boss the ends really do justify the means. To get $100m sales, a big bonus or a promotion your boss will be aggressive and sometimes walk all over you and your colleagues. Your boss probably believes in the philosophy that "being a good guy gets you nowhere." Bullies aren't "people pleasers" and usually don't work in customer-facing positions. They have a "get things done" attitude that is backed up by manipulative and aggressive behaviors.

Some bosses will be milder bullies in that they are pushy and political at work but not overly aggressive in their day-to-day dealings with subordinates.

Unappreciative

A frequent complaint about bosses is that they are unappreciative. You may work extra hours on a project and have it ready in tip-top shape but then the boss flicks through it with little enthusiasm, without voicing a single "thank you" or "well done" and passes on your next assignment. With time this lack of appreciation frustrates everyone, particularly those who crave positive feedback to feel fulfilled at work.

Control freak

This personality needs to have the say on everything that is done and control over every aspect of the tasks fulfilled in the workplace. From the choice of font on a report to the big decisions, this boss needs total control. The controlling boss has an eye on you and your work all day long and doesn't give you the space to be creative and enjoy your work. What motivates them is seeing a task completed to what they believe is perfection. Their "can do" attitude is both their greatest strength and weakness.

3.3   A general diagnosis of your relationship with your boss

Score each of the following indicators out of ten, where ten means totally true and zero means not true at all. Indicators that you must be working well with your boss:

☐ Gives you good performance appraisals and 360 scores.

☐ Is open, consistent and fair about your strengths and developmental needs.

☐ Understands what motivates you and uses this knowledge.

☐ Is as open with you as anyone else on his or her team.

☐ Involves you in new and challenging tasks or projects.

☐ Asks for your ideas or advice on certain issues – asking you good open questions.

☐ Rewards you fairly and favorably in terms of variable remuneration/bonus and base pay.

☐ Shares other opportunities with you and balances your developmental interests with the wider interests of the organization and his or her own needs and responsibilities (i.e., Is prepared to develop you and let you move onto other areas of the business).

☐ Treats you respectfully at all times.

☐ Shares information with you.

☐ Others recognize the quality of your working relationship.

☐   Confides in you.

☐   Your relationship has been tested in difficult moments and this is now a source of strength and resilience in the relationship.

☐   Is open and generous with their time with you, especially when you need it.

☐   Listens actively to you and does not interrupt too early.

☐   Gives you prompt and constructive feedback whether positive feedback or on something to improve.

Total score: _____

Maximum score: 160 points.

Score	Relationship diagnosis
135+	Great boss-employee relationship
110-134	Room for improvement, specific areas need improving
90-109	Plenty of room for improvement, some areas of relationship are in a poor state
0-89	Very poor relationship, significant changes required to improve overall relationship

Indicators that show you can improve your working relationship:

Your boss:

•   Low scores on some individual items in the previous assessment.

•   Something material or important feels unsaid or unspoken in the relationship.

•   The history of your relationship has not been easy and the challenges you both faced have not really bonded you closer.

You:

- Feeling uncomfortable or tense in your boss's presence.

- You may feel resistance to your boss's suggestions for your improvement or towards mentoring you.

- Feeling anxious generally in the presence of, or even just thinking about, people with authority.

- You think too much about how your boss may react instead of focusing on the task at hand.

3.4   Knowing the drivers of success in your boss's eyes

There are many situations here. Some leaders and managers make it abundantly clear what drives success in their eyes and what they expect from you both in objective results and also in terms of attitudes, values and behaviors. They will tell you. Some may take more of a joint win-win/negotiation type approach. Others seem to keep their distance and don't really open up, or if they do, they are stronger on discussing content than process, or vice versa.

In these later cases positive and open questioning skills can be very useful in creating open dialogue between you:

- What is most important here?

- Of these alternatives, which is of most value? What makes that so?

- What one or two things do you think I need to improve on to better help you and our team to be successful?

- Is there any way that I can better use my strengths in (insert skill) to help move this forward?

Understanding what your boss values is a fairly significant part of looking to improve your relationship with them. On the following page we have a self-assessment for you to compare your boss's values and what you need and value from your boss.

Boss value assessment

Score the following out of ten. How much does your boss a) value the following and b) value your own personal:

A   B

☐   ☐   Time

☐   ☐   Knowledge

☐   ☐   Skills

☐   ☐   Dependability

☐   ☐   Overall attitudes

☐   ☐   Loyalty

☐   ☐   Curiosity

☐   ☐   Pro-activity and ability to seek and take on new or wider responsibilities

☐   ☐   Humor

☐   ☐   Commitment

☐   ☐   Quality of work

☐   ☐   Contribution, results and outputs

How much do you a) need and b) value your boss for giving you:

A   B

☐   ☐   Healthy and valuable challenges

☐   ☐   Security

☐   ☐   Appreciation

☐   ☐   Wider recognition

☐   ☐   Training and developmental growth (or access thereto)

☐   ☐   Access to other opportunities

☐   ☐   General support

☐   ☐   Support at difficult times or in wider organizational conflict

☐   ☐   Advice

☐   ☐   Fair pay, benefits and bonus or variable pay*

☐   ☐   Tools and resources to do the job

*Note: Sometimes this is not fully under your boss's control. Please leave blank if this is the case.

3.5   Your boss's realities, strengths, weaknesses and preferences

It is important to know as much as possible about the realities, challenges, concerns and political positioning of your boss. Reflect and, if you can, share these factors with others in constructive discussions.

Observe and understand how your boss prefers to learn things – there is often a big difference in bosses who learn better from either reading or from listening. You need to know their preferences in communication for different types of issues – quantity, style, written and verbal etc. Reflect on how your boss remembers and learns best.

Always be prepared to ask about these preferences when you start up with a new boss. It is common to discuss "content" with new bosses – i.e., Objectives, business strategies and so on, but less common to discuss "process" – what, when and how in terms of communication.

Observe your boss's decision-making style – both at its best and when he or she seems to struggle, delay or lack judgment. How can you best leverage the strengths and mitigate the weaknesses? What do others do in this respect?

Use the space below to note any additional observations you have on your boss:

4. YOUR "A"

4.1   Look at yourself and your goals

Clearly there are two individuals in a relationship. They each have their needs, style, strong points and developmental issues. Then there is a space of interaction between them.

Part of the equation is to know yourself and what you bring to the relationship. Your boss's perception of what you bring to the relationship will be covered later.

A key aspect is how you act towards authority and different leadership and management styles. You may have a preference towards receiving a minimal, average or high level of control and direction from your boss. You may have picked up certain fears, inhibitions, trust, mistrust or reactions to authority from your early life. Indeed these can play out subconsciously throughout your life and can be difficult to change.

You need to be conscious and observant of how well your own behaviors, attitudes and actions play out with your boss. What works well? What seems to not work well?

_____

_____

_____

_____

Conflict is a key test of a relationship – i.e., When you disagree or need different things in a relationship. Learning how to overcome such barriers effectively can require a high level of self-awareness and communication skills. Some complex cases here are best dealt by seeking the support of a coach.

4.2   Political skills

Clearly, to have an effective relationship with your boss you need to understand the political environments of both yourself and your boss. To some extent you may have similar political challenges but you will have some different realities since you are at different levels with different peers and bosses.

Use the framework in the *A to B Guide to Office Politics* to map your differing political strengths and challenges.

Think creatively. How can you help your boss with his/her political needs and challenges? How can he or she help you?

_____

_____

_____

_____

_____

Ask your boss about what you can do that would be most useful and helpful. Ask for feedback on what you are doing well and what you could improve on in terms of your political savvy. Sometimes more valuable feedback is given in relaxed or even tense moments on a day-to-day basis than in the standard annual performance review. Indeed nothing new should appear at the annual review, it should be a good time to step back and look at the overall picture, but it is unlikely that new issues should be brought to the table at this time.

Often, delivering well on your agreed targets and goals is enough to help your boss gain political credibility. Sometimes, however, you can do a bit more by helping in an area of weaknesses or by giving feedback in a positive non-judgmental way. This will help your boss rationalize and seek new ways of doing things.

The *A to B Guide to Office Politics* can be a great source of advice and guidance in this area.

4.3   Your persuasive skills

There will be times when you disagree with your boss or wish to persuade them of an idea, business need or new way of doing things.

To be persuasive with a boss can demand careful thinking and preparation.

Who and how has someone persuaded your boss in the past?

_____

_____

_____

How does your boss like to receive information and ideas? How long do they like to think things over?

_____

_____

_____

_____

_____

Some bosses like things in writing, others prefer a verbal briefing. Some are convinced by logic or numbers. Others respond better to more emotional appeals around the needs of people. Some like lots of detail and others prefer focusing on the big picture. You will also find bosses who are more intuitive in their analysis and decision-making.

What are your strengths in persuasion? What kinds of people do you persuade most easily?

_____

_____

_____

_____

Are you better at persuading your direct reports, your superiors, your boss or your peers? How about your external contacts and clients?

_____

_____

_____

_____

What influencing styles can you see others practicing that seem more effective with each of those different groups? What does this information say about you and the others? What does it say you could be better at?

_____

_____

_____

_____

_____

_____

_____

_____

_____

_____

_____

Who you are trying to influence and what they value in the relationship can be vital to choosing the right form of persuasion:

- *Show compassion and respect* – Most people want to feel they are liked and respected for who they are. At times this is difficult but often if we really knew the genetics and experiences of what made someone as they are we would be more compassionate.

- *Exchange or "give and take"* – Often relationships are strengthened by mutual support and asking how you can help each other, then delivering.

- *Public commitment* – Sharing goals across the entire organization, or within the team, can motivate people to deliver and not let others down.

- *Perceived expertise* – People often listen and show deference to those perceived to be the expert on a subject.

- *Authority* – Everyone has their attitude to authority. Some are energized by it, others fearful while some are sceptical.

- *Scarcity* – Some people will be more easily persuaded if they believe something is scarce – i.e., A rare opportunity.

- *Rules and standards* – Compliance is an important motivator for some.

- *Assertion* – Clear and articulate argument that is never aggressive.

- *Personal magnetism and charisma* – Some are more energized and attracted to this than others.

- *Visioning* – Some are able to paint a wonderful and motivating vision with well chosen words, a metaphor or story.

- *Bridging and consensus* – Some are attracted to the approach of carrying everyone forward together. Bosses often have different tolerances, skills and patience towards building consensus. Of course it can also depend upon the issue, its importance and urgency.

- *Joint problem solving* – The act of working through a problem with someone can be very powerful. You can either be contributing to or facilitating a solution.

It is imperative to know what you are best at and what forms most influence your boss. You may be able to use your strength with someone who in turn is better positioned to influence your boss. Indeed, sometimes the messenger is key.

Showing a interest in others and bonding over commonalities helps. You can ask people about what gives them the highest positive level of energy. This will give you great clues about their interests and passions.

4.4   Your level of confidence

Confidence can be critical to an effective and trusting relationship.

It is not uncommon for individuals to lack some confidence in dealing with certain types of bosses. Some we will feel very comfortable with and others very uncomfortable. The uncomfortable relationships can be turned into a great opportunity to grow your zone of comfort and self-confidence.

How would you describe your confidence? Does it fail you in certain situations? If so, describe when.

_____

_____

_____

_____

_____

See later for tips on expanding your comfort zone and confidence.

4.5   Perception of your boss and those around you

Sometimes we get frustrated because we think we are trying hard and doing the right things but others just seem to see things in a different way.

We hear it said in business that customer perception is critical. How people perceive brands may sometimes not seem logical, but they can be very loyal to a brand and their perception of that brand. Perceptions others have of you can work in a similar way.

How would you describe your personal brand? Do others view it as positive or negative?

_____

_____

_____

_____

_____

So if the perception of key people around you is positive and working well, congratulations. But what if you want to change or improve a perception? There are a number of tactics and tips in section 8.

4.6   Understanding yourself

Knowing ourselves well helps us to understand our own values, needs, strengths and weaknesses, as well as our personal style and how others perceive us. This will help you understand what aspects of your character, personality and abilities help your relationship with your boss to be effective and what might have a negative or suboptimal impact on it.

For example, a subordinate may feel too strongly that they need to show competence and therefore that they are "in the right." Their need to be right is too pushy and keeps them pressing forward with their argument. The more they feel they are not winning the argument the harder they try. This can lead to an unnecessary escalation of tension and disagreement.

The situation may be different with peers who sense the commitment and strength of an argument, but for the boss it can come across as defiance. In such situations it can be important for the individual to receive constructive feedback and questioning as to how they could improve, what alternative influencing strategies might work better etc.

A boss-subordinate relationship is based on mutual dependence. But in truth a subordinate is often more dependent on the boss. This is often due to level of authority, decision making power or level, experience and political influence.

It is natural and often based on early experiences and parental attitudes to authority that we all have differing attitudes to authority ourselves. Some grow up resenting authority, some are fearful, rebellious, compliant, sceptical and some have a generally healthy and open minded approach. These attitudes can be mild or really embedded. Think about your early life and what you were told, what your relationships were like with your parents and early teachers.

Write down a list of the first ten to fifteen words or expressions that come to mind when you think of bosses and people in authority.

_____

_____

_____

_____

_____

_____

_____

What do these words say about your experiences and feelings? Are these positive or negative? What is the balance? Do some of the negatives reflect on you and our own experiences more than on authority in general?

Do you need to be more conscious of such feelings and make more effort to look at the positive aspects and strengths of the individuals in authority around you?

Remember also that your boss will have had his or her own early experiences and difficulties with authority figures. This could play out in several ways but when we think of some of our own difficult experiences and their impact on ourselves it helps us to have more compassion and understanding for our boss.

Overall, our attitudes to authority can be reflected in how our behaviors shift along the scale of unassertive to assertive and then on to aggressive. These can be complex in that, for example, your boss may have difficulty with people superior to them (i.e., By being compliant and unassertive), but may be open and accepting in dealing with subordinates. Other bosses may be unassertive and highly supportive with their bosses but aggressive with subordinates. It helps to know both your own style and your boss's approach. The ideal is that you can both be assertive, trusting and open and can find win-win solutions together.

5. LOOKING AT YOUR "A" FROM A NEW PERSPECTIVE

Here you will find a group of techniques to help you make deeper observations and seek improvements that use the power of your mind. You may find some techniques more useful than others based on your personality type but give them a try. Hopefully you'll be surprised with what you've discovered at the end of the process.

5.1   Techniques for delving deeper

a)   NLP meta mirror

    i)   Imagine a common meeting with your boss. Are you sitting or standing? Take up whichever position you decide. Imagine your boss across from you. Try to recreate the situation as closely as possible – for example, place an empty chair behind a desk and imagine your boss sitting there. Think of a challenging issue or previous conversation between the two of you. Ask yourself, "What am I experiencing, thinking and feeling as I look at my boss?"

    ii)   Now shake that off and place yourself where your boss "appeared." Look back at yourself through your bosses eyes and ask yourself the same question, "What am I experiencing, thinking and feeling as I look at my subordinate (yourself)?"

    iii)   Now shake that off and stand in a third position to the side. Look at the situation and the relationship and what each person is experiencing, thinking and feeling. Be an impartial observer. You might even imagine yourself being someone you know is wise, calm, analytical and detached.

    iv)   Now shake that off and stand in another place, the fourth position. Think about how your thoughts in the third position compared to your reactions in the first position. Switch them around.

v)   Now go back and revisit the second position. Ask yourself: "How is this different now?" and "What has changed?"

vi)   Finish by returning to the first position. Ask yourself: "How is this different now?" and "What has changed?"

This technique has been shown to be powerful with difficult bosses, for example, the bully type.

b)   Getting feedback from others

We can use the perspectives of others to help us see things differently. Choose a good time and a relaxed situation to ask somebody whose opinions you value as being impartial and well-judged. Ask open questions, for example: How do you see our (you and the boss) working relationship? What do you think works well in it? What do you think could be improved? Do you have any suggestions for what I could do differently in the future to help in this respect?

360 feedback instruments can be a very useful way of receiving impartial and helpful feedback. Many companies are using these now.

c)   Visual techniques

Sometimes when we are struggling to find answers, visual techniques can be extremely helpful.

Try to sketch a picture of your relationship with your boss on a blank piece of paper. What features are most pronounced? Now take another blank piece of paper and sketch out your ideal boss relationship. What is most marked in this sketch? Overall, what changes are you looking for?

An alternative to sketching is to find photographs or pieces of art that express your feelings about your actual and ideal relationships with your boss.

d)   The boss's shoes

Really take some time to think through the pressures your boss experiences, both inside and outside work. How much do you really understand about what drives your boss's behaviors and reactions? How much do you know about their formative years? Conclude by thinking how much you know and how much you've done. What assumptions have you been making?

e)   Different hats

Imagine you could use different hats that induced different thinking and different perspectives. As in the NLP meta mirror, imagine being an outsider looking at the relationship. Think as:

* A cynic.

* A negative person.

* A positive/optimistic person.

* A generous and sympathetic person who sees the good in everyone.

* A highly creative person full of new ideas and alternative strategies.

* A risk-averse and highly cautious person.

* A pragmatic realist.

What new aspects did you learn?

_____

_____

_____

f)   Listen to the music

Many people find music extremely powerful. Here you can imagine a piece of music that expresses the feelings present in a relationship. As with the visualization technique, it can be helpful to also think about a piece of music that expresses what you would like to happen to the relationship.

You can then "play" your preferred piece in your mind when you want to attain a certain energy and emotional state during a tough situation with your boss. You might also want to use this technique before important meetings or encounters.

g)   Finding the metaphor

Seek a metaphor that best describes your boss's leadership style or your relationship with your boss. What ideas can you draw from this metaphor?

For example, say your metaphor for your boss is: "My boss is like a charging bull." How about observing when your boss is calmer and more approachable? What things or situations flip your boss from calm to "charging bull" mode? When your boss is charging at full force what is the best strategy? Should you move aside or attempt to tranquilize the "bull?"

h)   Find the storyline

Imagine you are writing a novel. Write the story of your relationship so far. What do you notice? What were the first impressions you had of each other? How did things progress? What were pivotal or key moments in the relationship and how were they interpreted by these two different "characters." What ways can the story get to a better place? What might prove transformational in the story going forward? How could that be engineered?

6. What Might your Ideal "B" Look Like?

6.1   Ideal boss relationships

Now that you have analyzed and reflected more on your boss, yourself and your relationship you can start to think about what **B** might look like. Ideally **B** would be a "win-win-win relationship" – you both support and challenge each other in the right way and measure for your personalities, needs and reasonable expectations. This would help both of you achieve your immediate and longer-term personal objectives and job tasks efficiently and effectively. These also would produce results that are aligned with your organization's needs, strategy, vision and values. Therefore, a skilled subordinate will have a positive mentality and be looking for win-win-win solutions for themselves, the teams they work in and their boss.

Ideal relationships usually involve trust, respect, openness, honesty, understanding, knowledge, effective and timely communication as well as the right degree of challenge and mutual support. Such qualities will help make the relationship effective, efficient and sustainable. Each will help bring out the best in the other and the relationship will be energizing.

6.2   Other clues for you to consider

Who was the best boss you ever had? What made them so? What does this say about your development preferences?

_____

_____

_____

_____

Conversely, who was the worst boss you ever had? What made them so? What does this say about your potential development needs?

_____

_____

_____

_____

Always remember that the toughest bosses can often offer you the most personal growth. Who finds them a much better boss than you do? What is the difference? This may reveal a potential weakness in your armory as you try to move forward. For example, some bosses are aggressive and tough. They may like and respect people who push back and challenge them (they might not!). If you lack the courage to push back even when you want to, it may be that you need to grow in assertiveness or strengthen your ability to deal positively with conflict.

6.3   Pulling your self-assessments together

Go through your notes and answers to sections 3, 4 and 5.

Brainstorming an ideal **B** helps us put developing our boss relationship in context and think creatively about what might be good to prioritize in improving that working relationship.

What do you want to get from a better relationship with your boss? Improved career prospects, less stress, more fun, pet project approval, more power and resources? Take your time to write down what YOU want to gain from this:

Review your answers from sections 3, 4 and 5. Summarize your answers to each section for the questions provided below on a) your boss' support and challenge, b) yourself and c) your relationship with your boss:

a)   Your boss

Based on what you've analyzed so far what does your boss do best in being your boss?

_____

_____

_____

_____

What could your boss do better in being your boss?

_____

_____

_____

_____

Using your two previous answers describe your ideal boss for the job you are in:

_____

_____

_____

_____

b)   Yourself

What are your own strengths in dealing with bosses?

_____

_____

_____

_____

What are your development needs in dealing with bosses?

_____

_____

_____

_____

Combine your two answers to describe your ideal vision for yourself: In dealing with bosses, I will be...

_____

_____

_____

_____

c)   Your relationship with your actual boss

What are the strengths of your relationship?

_____

_____

_____

_____

In what ways does your relationship need to develop?

_____

_____

_____

_____

When my relationship with my boss is ideal it will be...

_____

_____

_____

_____

7. YOUR A TO B

Now we turn to using your creative thinking inspired by "the ideal."

We often need to come down to ground level and think what our ideal means in reality. What are pragmatic and realistic steps? What is in the "too difficult" box? Can we separate first steps, short term goals and longer term objectives? The rest of this guidebook will focus on the practical world of change and give you the support to make change happen.

7.1   Making change happen

There are three main classifications of change here:

*   Aspects you have to work on yourself.

*   Aspects your boss may need to develop or change.

*   Aspects you both need to work on together.

There are many permutations and possible areas of change so here are some general tips for each:

a)   Aspects you need to work on yourself

Typically these can involve things like:

*   A negative or insecure attitude towards authority.

*   Changes to help you be more effective given your boss's work, delegation and communication strengths and preferences.

*   Changes in your communication to help you have a greater impact and get more focus or air time from your boss.

*   Improvements in your attitudes, dependability, etc.

Remember your boss can help you prioritize these. A good open question to your boss can be "If I could improve two or three things to help better support you and the department (or team etc.), what do you think

I should prioritize?" This invitation to improve your support to your boss will be received positively by many bosses.

b)   Change isn't easy

Changing your boss is often a difficult task! The tips in the next section help you consider how you can go about this. Some bosses may ask for feedback and show real concern for your views and commit to working on your feedback. It might be that your boss asks for feedback but is too busy or finds changing deceptively difficult. He or she may need the support of a skilled coach. You may even have open support from your HR contact for this. At other times your boss may not be looking for feedback and can be resistant to change. We'll investigate how to deal with this later.

c)   General relationship issues

Sometimes there is an overall relationship issue. For example, the trust between both of you may have diminished due to an incident or differing viewpoint. Or you may have been getting more distant over time as other priorities led your boss away from contact with you. Here you might be able to get recognition of the issue and brainstorm a practical way of addressing the issue that is also a "win" for the needs and goals of the department.

7.2   Tougher aspects to change

Things that are generally harder to change can be cultural, ingrained and natural personality traits.

Perhaps you uncovered some issues from the self-awareness questions in section 4 and then you used the increased self-awareness to try to make a shift. Then you tried some of the techniques in section 5 to see things from a new perspective and to help you change. What if you know what you need to change but something seems to hold you back from making progress?

Well, it is more common than you might think that the "little voice" in our head can limit our self-belief or ability to act effectively. This is sometimes referred to as our subconscious or unconscious mind. Things we experience in our formative years can sit deep in certain places within our minds and sabotage our behavior at certain moments. This is often the case with our attitudes to authority and control – we are exposed to many early experiences of authority through our parents and early teachers or other authority figures. Sometimes our parents have strong views on authority figures at work or in society that we take on board at a young and impressionable age. These can then influence our deeper feelings and beliefs later on.

One of my coaching clients described how a single incident when his father reprimanded him publicly after he made a mistake and dropped something had a pivotal effect ever since on his view of authority. It later affected his ability to form positive relationships with his bosses.

Our rational conscious minds might know what is better, but something stronger and deeper can kick in through our emotions. The good news is that there are techniques to help us!

Change here can be difficult unless we use tools and techniques that work for the parts of the brain that don't always react to words, logic or being told what to do by the rational brain. Remember, the brain is modular – with different parts and different functions. If you need further help, consider reaching out to a mentor or coach as they will likely be able to accelerate your progress and assist you in overcoming complex stumbling blocks you may encounter.

8. Personal Change – General Tips

a) Tuning-in to what motivates you

What motivates you? When have you felt most energized in your career and work? What do these moments, periods, assignments or projects tell you about what motivates you?

How can you link these things to your change plan and efforts?

If, for example, you are motivated by new challenges, link the need for your changes to getting your boss to open new doors and future new and exciting challenges.

b) Be positive in goal setting

We cannot grow less of a negative thing very effectively. We can grow something we value and find positive much more easily. Goals with a negative in them don't tend to work too well. Indeed negatively expressed goals can backfire as the mind tends to focus on the concept involved, whether or not the word "no" or "not" precedes it.

c) Have a plan

A well-thought-out plan that you find exciting can make all the difference. A format is given to you in the Appendix section of this guidebook. Breaking an objective down into simple steps can make the difficult seem easier.

d) Stretch out of your comfort zone in successive smaller steps

Think of your **A** as your comfort zone. **B** might be quite a stretch for you. So a good strategy is to be creative in designing small successive expansions to your comfort zone. Then you can grow in confidence and plan realistic steps. Overstretching out of your comfort zone can lead you to struggling and wanting to forget about change.

f) Do it early

Aim to do the actions that stretch your comfort zone early in your day.

Then you can ride the positive energy from the achievement throughout the day rather than leaving it until later and carrying it in the back of your mind all day.

g)   Hold yourself accountable

To change we often need something that or someone who helps us stay on track. Who can you show your goals and targets to and would be good at following up to see whether you are completing the actions needed? What other incentives might help you?

h)   Look at your goals daily

First thing every working day you can look at something visual that reminds you of what you are working towards. It could be the picture of a role model for the aspect you are working on or a scene that expresses where you want to get to. Looking at these pictures intently on a daily basis for a few minutes really can help drive the energy and focus you need to change.

So be creative in capturing your goals in emotionally positive ways.

This could include creating a storyline or narrative that you find inspiring. You can also create metaphors that encapsulate the change you are trying to make.

i)   Celebrate victories

Of course! With whom and how?

j)   Get the support you need

Work out the resources you need to best support you – the who, what and how.

This can include ongoing feedback, perhaps a developmental course, experience, mentoring or coaching.

k)   Leverage your strengths

Always try to use the best resources you have. Be creative in thinking through how you can use your talents and learning preferences to better support yourself.

l)   Have fun

We learn better and faster when we are having fun. What can you do that integrates something you find fun with your developmental challenge?

Learn to lighten up at times and to see the funny side too.

m)   Changing perceptions and managing expectations

Sometimes your boss may have arrived at a perception of you that gets a bit ingrained. Perceptions can come from single occurrences and out-of-context or unusual circumstances.

So sometimes they are not very balanced but they can be hard to shift!

If your boss seems to have an unfair perception of you, here are some tips to help you change it:

- After discussing some positive things and your boss is not rushed, ask what he or she thinks about your (insert subject). Make sure it is focused on their perception and kept in the most objective business-like terms possible.

- Ask what you could do differently in future.

- Perhaps ask if they could support you in this improvement and give you ongoing feedback. Ask: "Can you help me and give me feedback on how I am doing as I try to implement that change?"

These simple steps can be very powerful as they show your boss that you are conscious of an issue, keen to change and that you value your boss's opinion and support. Now your boss really knows that you are concerned, willing to change and have asked them for THEIR advice and support. Unfortunately perceptions are so often left untouched!

Sometimes you may need a respected ally who is influential with the other person to put in a good word that will begin to change someone's perception.

Sometimes you can experiment with changes in the area of perception difficulty and see what seems to cause a paradigm shift in the person's reaction and achieve a "wow – I didn't expect that!" type of reaction.

Don't be upset if you are not perceived the way you would like to be. Frequently people have preferences or values that make it difficult for you to succeed. There can be times after trying in good faith when you need to value yourself and who you truly are as a person and make a call as to whether to continue as best you can or to seek "new pastures."

n)   Expand your comfort zone and build confidence

There are several ways of boosting your self-confidence and expanding your comfort zone:

- Trying something new on a regular basis, each step carefully designed to take you just a little bit further.

- Trying something new in a risk-free environment.

- Role-play tough situations with a friend, mentor or coach. Role-playing can expand your horizons and help you see things from others' perspectives. The best bit is that you can get instant feedback from the person supporting you.

- Putting yourself in your boss's shoes. This can include being compassionate enough to understand why he or she acts and behaves in certain ways.

- Truly understanding what you value and what you want, and therefore, what battles you may need to face up to and those that you should let go of. Prioritizing here can be important.

These simple steps can be very powerful as they show your boss that you are conscious of an issue, keen to change and value your boss's opinion and support. Instead of allowing things to remain unspoken, take this approach as a powerful beginning to transforming negative perceptions.

9. A TO B OF DEALING WITH DIFFICULT BOSSES

The following are strategies for coping with the boss personality types mentioned in section 3:

9.1   Indecisive bosses

It is very easy to get annoyed with indecisive people but approaching them in an impatient or aggressive manner will get you nowhere with them. Pushing indecisive bosses into making decisions often causes them to push back and try to procrastinate, maybe even create new alternatives to consider. Anger will also work against you both on a political and personal level.

Indecisive bosses are afraid of committing to something that may be viewed later as a terrible mistake. Hence, you must build trust with them by being patient and sensitive to their circumstances and feelings. You also must make it your objective to help your boss improve his/her decision-making abilities.

So to teach your boss how to make decisions you need to start with the basic building blocks of trust and comfort. Indecisive bosses usually like everyone to get along and are quite risk-averse individuals. You must create an open channel of communication with your boss. Reassure him/her that despite the tough decision they can express their concerns with you in confidence. Be careful with your tone of voice and facial expressions. Make sure you convey sincerity and are open and warm in your approach.

Sample conversation:

"Kevin, how are things going with the decision on our new product line?" Dave says to his boss.

"Well Dave, I'm still thinking about it." the boss replies in his typical indecisive manner.

"It's not an easy decision, but we need to come up with our final decision soon. I'm sure you're taking your time for a good reason. Is there something that's on your mind about the whole thing? You know you can talk to me about it." Dave responds in an open, friendly way.

The boss opens up, "The things on my mind are..."

Notice how Dave approaches his boss without accusations or judgment, but instead showing understanding and warmth. Notice also the clever use of "we need to come up with our final decision" instead of "you." Indecisive people respond badly to pushiness. By building some rapport with the boss, Dave was able to open up his boss to discussing what his mental blocks are with the decision at hand.

Now that you have managed to get your boss to open up a bit try to get them to reveal what is holding back their decision. Is there some conflict in their mind? Do they have any fears? Are they concerned about your reaction, their boss's reaction or your peers' reaction?

Once you have found out what the conflict, issue, or fear they have is, help them develop a decision-making method. Indecisive bosses probably aren't good at mentally deciding between their options so writing out a decision plan can work well. For some people a simple chart with the options divided into columns to compare the positives and negatives of each choice works for them.

Option 1	Option 2	Option 3
Positives	Positives	Positives
Negatives	Negatives	Negatives

Others may still struggle to weigh positives and negatives so perhaps a number weighted decision chart would work better. For instance, for every positive implication give a score of 1 to 10. For every negative implication score it -1 to -10. Add up the scores and the best option will usually be the one with the highest score. Of course an option with too many high negatives could be withdrawn altogether, that depends on their judgement. But don't motivate your boss into further indecision and procrastination by highlighting this. Try to get them to follow a method that works and help them to stick to it.

Once your boss has managed to make a decision based on the method you've introduced, assure them they have made a good decision. Decisions won't always be perfect but with enough consideration and a good decision-making method your boss will do well. Let them know this.

Don't let them fall into old habits and procrastinate. Make sure they follow through with their decision and implement it. Give them the assurance they need to turn their decisions into reality.

You've done it! Your boss now feels more confident with making decisions and will trust you and appreciate you for what you've done for them. As long as you keep them in check and continue to build a stronger relationship, you'll have a decisive boss who is more likely to give you a raise than frustrate you!

9.2   Self-centered bosses

The immediate reaction most people have to an egotistical person is to try and "knock them off their throne" by making negative remarks about them. This is not a constructive idea however, especially with your superior. Here we'll cover some techniques to help you get your ideas across to a boss who always thinks they are right!

*   ***Knowledge & confidence*** – Egotistical bosses think they know their stuff much better than others, are superior in intellect/knowledge/abilities to their subordinates and therefore are often quickly dismissive of your ideas. When you are discussing something they can at times focus more on the negative aspects, lapses in logic and misguided facts within your ideas. The number one tool is to be prepared and confident in your capabilities.

    If you are presenting a set of data for instance, understand how you reached all figures, how these figures may be perceived and be prepared to make comments and suggestions on every piece of data. One incorrect or badly explained response and your boss could dismiss all your work during the meeting. Don't give your boss that window! When you know the facts, understand the rationale behind the facts, have thought about possible criticisms of your ideas and prepared responses/solutions to these, you can grow in confidence with your assertions. A confident and knowledgeable you makes it difficult for a know-it-all egotistical boss to thwart your ideas.

*   ***Show you are listening*** – It's not uncommon to show in our responses and expressions that we immediately disagree with an egotistical per-

son's thoughts. This won't get them to agree with what you are about to say. So the way to begin to engage in manifesting your differing views is to listen and show you are listening both verbally and non-verbally. While your boss is speaking, show you are listening with an open and interested posture. While listening you can occasionally nod to show you have understood or say something like "OK" or "I understand" or "I see where you are coming from with this idea" all with a positive tone and emphasis. Tone is hugely important as all these quotes can sound dismissive or sarcastic if not spoken with sincerity and a positive attitude. Then, as you are about to express your point of view, repeat some of the key aspects of your boss's ideas. Don't feel as if you are stroking their ego, merely showing you have understood and listened and are looking to build a positive bridge between their point of view and yours. You want them to collaborate with your idea, not fight against it, so do the same.

- *Understand your boss's criteria* – For your boss to believe in his/her idea there has to be certain criteria that are important to them that their idea satisfies. When you understand what is important to your boss on a conceptual level you can address doubts he/she may have about the quality and viability of your ideas. In the past what have been reasons your boss has used to ignore/disregard your ideas? This will give you some clues as to what your boss finds important. You may find that a few statements your boss makes in response to your previous discussions are repetitive. Learn from this. You can start to move forward by showing them the respect of listening to and acknowledging their ideas first then showing them how your ideas meet their criteria and address their frequent doubts.

Say, for instance, your boss finds your ideas will always cost too much. Before introducing your idea fully say something along the lines of: "As we are looking to build business without hiking costs too much…" If time is the issue then something like "As a team we have little time on our hands, that is why I thought we could maybe…"

- *Present your ideas/views softly* – Now that you've been patient and done the legwork to get your boss to listen to you without raising their defences, you should present your ideas/views slowly and softly. Expressions like "maybe we could…" or "perhaps we could" or "I was wondering if we did…" you will make your ideas sound less challenging to the egomaniac boss. The hypothetical nature of your idea presentation gives your boss a chance to consider it and almost make the idea seem like it's his/hers. Ask questions to get your boss in a thinking state. Perhaps they will even come up with a new dimension to your idea. If they give good answers and suggestions be encouraging as this will increase the likelihood they will play ball with your idea. Be patient and not aggressive. If they begin to take ownership of your initial idea, don't feel disheartened, take it as a compliment to your newfound persuasive abilities!

- *Acknowledge their good ideas* – You don't have to suck up to your egotistical boss to do well. If your boss does in fact come up with a good idea, acknowledge it, show your desire to know more and learn from them. When you build a relationship where your boss begins to feel like a mentor, you create trust. When you want to make a change or a move you may find a more receptive and less self-absorbed boss.

9.3   Bullying bosses

The tendency most people have with bullying bosses is to counter-attack, defend or withdraw entirely. Unfortunately, none of these immediate reactions work. Attacking back with the same aggressiveness as your boss will only escalate problems. Playing defensive by making excuses and justifying yourself simply falls on deaf ears and tends to incite more bullying. By withdrawing you show weakness and this is something a bully loves as it justifies their behavior and gives them the feeling of superiority they seek. What you have to do instead is command respect.

By showing a bullying boss you are strong, confident and assertive he/she will begin to respect you and tone down aggressive behavior. This isn't the easiest of tasks but you are capable of standing your ground and here is how to go about doing that:

When being attacked by your bullying boss keep your calm and control. Don't run and don't attack. Just maintain your posture, look directly at your boss and keep your calm. This simple non-verbal act conveys you are in control and undaunted by your boss's behavior. This says to your boss "I'm in control, doing my job as best as I can, getting my work done while you are behaving this way!", without having to say a word! Especially if you are new to the job you don't want to be overly verbal, but your self-control will speak volumes.

Sometimes you may need to call your boss's attention. While he/she is in attack mode one technique is to repeat their name several times until they calm down and you've got their attention. You don't want to be shouting their name or sounding aggressive, but instead appear assertive and calm.

"Monica, Monica, Monica," you begin to say assertively.

The boss's aggression continues, "I'm trying to make our company profitable and you are doing nothing!"

"Monica, Monica, Monica," you continue.

Once you've got their attention quickly show you've been paying attention to what he/her had to say:

"I understand you are trying to increase our profitability…"

Then quickly get to the root of your argument and express your point of view. Bullies are impatient and ready to keep firing at you so make it short and sweet:

"In my opinion we need to focus first on marketing our company better before we address the issue of profitability. I've prepared a report for you that deals with these issues."

Now is the time to end the argument in an assertive way that lets your boss know their behavior isn't going to work with you.

"I'm happy to share my report with you and discuss this further when you are ready to speak to me with respect."

Yes, this may sound a little aggressive to you but to a bully you come across as assertive and a reasonable person – you listen to him/her, he/ she respects you and your opinion and therefore you both can discuss how to move forward.

If you are in a situation where your boss is bullying you for something you have done wrong you should admit your mistake, show what you have learned from the mistake and say how you will change to prevent such a mistake from happening again. It is particularly important you state how you will prevent the mistake from resurfacing as it will stop your boss from attacking you further.

9.4   Unappreciative bosses

A boss may have many reasons for not showing appreciation for you and your work. They may have trouble expressing feelings, want to avoid inflating employees' egos or feel they are too busy in between tasks to "give time to compliments." Whatever your boss's thinking or reasons may be there are a few things you should look to understand about this kind of relationship.

*   Just because your boss hasn't verbally acknowledged your effort doesn't mean he/she doesn't appreciate it. If your boss is highly critical you should take some comfort in the fact he/she hasn't made negative remarks about your work as per usual.

    Some bosses show appreciation in their expression more than they do verbally. They may look pleasantly surprised but not want to say so. Give yourself a pat on the back if this happens, you've done well, it's just not your boss's style to compliment others.

*   Ask them for feedback. If they don't express gratitude then ask them what they thought of your work. Be prepared for possible criticism but rejoice any positive observations.

*   Unappreciative bosses won't gel well with employees who constantly seem needy for compliments. You should look to build your confidence and understand that your boss's personality means they are highly scrutinizing, but that it doesn't mean your work is paltry.

*   Listen to their criticisms of you. Next time you meet or present something to your boss show that you are working on those issues. With time they will hopefully warm to you as you have shown respect for their opinions. This might make it easier for them to open up and praise you.

*   Suppose you've been working very hard and saving your boss's ass. If it's convenient, consider taking a holiday break from work. In all of our relationships in life, sometimes people need to miss us a little before they learn to appreciate us more. Hopefully when you return to the office you'll have new energy to deal with your boss and they

are more appreciative of your contribution to the company.

9.5   Control freak bosses

The control freak boss likes getting things done. They want to see action and results and frequently take matters into their own hands. Some of the characteristics of a control freak can be good for a business if used in moderation when a team needs strong leadership. It's when your boss can't ever let go of control that there can be a serious problem. This can occur because your boss has trust issues, enjoys the feeling of power that constant control gives them, feels superior or has fears of failure. If your boss falls into the category of control due to the superiority complex then look at the advice for self-centered bosses. Otherwise let's tackle these root causes...

A controlling boss with trust issues and a fear of failure has to be dealt with by addressing your relationship and your boss's perception of you as an employee. Earlier in this guidebook you were asked to investigate the perception your boss and others have of you. Are current perceptions favorable? Are you regarded as responsible, hardworking, attentive, goal-oriented or knowledgeable? If you aren't seen as any of these you have to begin re-branding yourself. Build a reputation of trustworthiness by delivering on promises be them big or small. Show you are hardworking by going above and beyond expectations to deliver quality work. Show attentiveness by not letting small details pass you by. Develop a passion for achieving your targets and getting those around you onboard too. As mentioned in previous sections, know your stuff. A boss won't trust someone they feel is ill-prepared to handle the workload.

You also have to build trust by maintaining an open relationship with your boss. Offer them assistance on tasks. If they refute your attempts, explain that you feel capable of executing the task and would enjoy executing it. Perhaps even challenge your boss: "I would really like to do X, I feel I am capable because of Y and Z. Give me an opportunity to prove to you I'm capable, if things don't work out I will let you carry on doing it." If your boss accepts your offer then make sure you do your utmost to successfully complete the task because you probably will only be given one chance! Results will speak for themselves and build a platform for trust.

If power-hungriness is more of the issue you might have to concede more control to your boss once you've been given the green-light to deliver on a task. Perhaps suggest daily/weekly check-up meetings or progress reports with your boss so they feel they aren't losing total control over a project while giving you the space to execute things. If you find your boss getting in the way even after you've agreed to a reporting system reinforce the fact they have nothing to worry about and that things are under control. You want to get your boss off your case but without being rude or aggressive, so be smooth. Explain that any doubts/suggestions/ advice they have can be discussed at your next meeting as you would be more concentrated to listen to each other and could discuss all issues in more depth. You want to show you value their insights but that now isn't a good time for their intervention.

10. TIPS FOR IMPROVING YOUR RELATIONSHIP

10.1 Pushing back

You know what your organization and team need to achieve and have your own interpretation of what is in the stakeholders' best interests. Perhaps there is an approach your boss is taking that you don't agree with. It could be a "hard" difference – i.e., A difference in opinion about a strategy, plan, process, etc. Or it could be a difference in relation to a "soft" issue – for example, a team leadership or influencing style.

Whether or not to push back and, if so, how hard to push back, is an important consideration. There are many factors at play and there are risks too. Some bosses do not accept pushing back well. Others almost encourage it. So here can be a real test of your judgment – assessing the issue, the different opinions, the importance, the risk, the style and concerns of your boss and the organizational politics etc.

Given the risks, you may need to think through how to escalate the issue gradually without overexposing yourself. It's often really helpful to think through questions you can make that give you clues as to your boss's preferences and decision factors. You can even put questions in a positive way. For example, "I can see clear advantages of X [your boss's view]. What do you think are the pros and cons of doing Y?" If your boss is being very aggressive and bad-tempered with an individual and you wish to call him/her on this behavior you may say: "In the meeting today the atmosphere was tense. We are all pulling for the success of the team, but my perception was morale dipped after the meeting. How can we best help you deliver the results and keep morale up?"

As far as possible it is good to stick to facts. This becomes more difficult when the issue is your boss's behaviors and their impact on yourself or the team. It's always good to check with others whether they share your views or feelings. Choose people that can help give you a reality check – on your logic, assumptions or conclusions. You may also need to judge how much time the issue merits analysis. Some issues carry a higher risk and importance than others.

Sometimes your boss has behaviors, views, practices or makes decisions that you find unacceptable.

In such cases you have a range of options including:

- Accepting things and "let it go."

- Trying to subtly influence changes or compromises through others. Also using influencing approaches such as questions.

- Making clear you disagree or would have preferred another course, but will support 100%.

- Pushing back harder – deciding this is a battle to fight.

- Leaving or getting a transfer.

You may need to consider the "political web" and issues like timing. Pushing back firmly can be a high-risk strategy. Your boss may find it a threat. It might be in an area of insecurity that means they feel they need to resist or push back even firmer, using the authority of their position. Ultimately this could result in you losing your job.

Some national and corporate cultures have a greater propensity to allow people to challenge the boss. These are sometimes referred to as low-power distance cultures. In higher-power distance cultures you are more likely to hear expressions like "the boss is the boss" or "what the boss says goes!" So these factors can have a big influence on the level of risk involved.

Escalating things to your boss's boss or one of your boss's superiors can bring your loyalty into question and the dynamics of power can some-times make it a no-win situation. If you decide to go this way you may need to think about your exit or back-up strategy.

Always remember you can develop a menu of levels of assertiveness in making your point. It is very rare that aggression and anger are appropri-ate. You can escalate things more subtly at first by asking open questions, testing the "temperature" or the views from above. But remember also that when you skip a level, what you say can get relayed word for word to your direct boss, or perhaps even worse, they can be misinterpreted and distorted.

Checklist for pushing back

- Have I cross-checked my facts?

- Have I cross-checked my thinking and assumptions with trusted peers?

- Is it a question of saying "no?" How can I best phrase my "no?" Can I learn from other occasions in which other staff have said "no" with minimum negative impact? Can I offer an acceptable alternative?

- Can I break the issue down and try for a smaller "win?" Can I use lateral thinking and repackage the issue into an area my boss is committed or favorable to? What is most likely to get my boss truly listening? How can I avoid sounding like a broken record?

- How is my boss likely to react? Have I truly put myself in their shoes? Do I really understand their personality, values, priorities and the pressures upon them?

- What are the political dynamics over the issue? Do I understand the power dynamics? Have I mapped the political web around the issue?

- What are the risks and worst case scenarios of pushing back?

- How can I mitigate such risks? Can I float ideas first? Can I use open questions?

- Who is the best messenger for this message? Is it me or is it better coming from someone else who has a greater chance of being respected and listened to?

- What are the best tactics? If I approach my boss what is the best timing and place? Is my boss more receptive when in certain moods or after good news? Do I know where and when my boss is most receptive? Is it on the golf course?!

10.2   Solving other common mistakes

- *Time in the office* – There are company cultures where it is expected that people who are looking for a promotion need to be seen by their bosses as early starters and late finishers. The key is to not assume that if others are doing this that it may be true. Ask your boss what's most important. Let your boss know, sometimes subtly, that you worked at home, for example: "I managed to finish the report off at home. It took me several hours, but I was able to go at it uninterrupted and I'm pleased with the result." Remember though that your boss may sound supportive but sometimes there are almost subconscious cultural decisions being made about your fit if your hours don't meet the normal unspoken expectations. Look at who got the last promotions.

- *Remember some things can't wait* – When there is bad news, delays and hesitations are often not the best course of action. You may wish to wait for your boss to be in a more positive mood, but things can get even worse if your boss learns from someone else and you were sitting on something under your responsibility.

- *Take care bashing the boss behind his/her back* – You never know who will report back when you dish out gossip or bad-mouth your boss. If in doubt, it's best to stick with the positive. When others do it consider saying "yes, but..." and mentioning one of the boss's strengths.

- *Focus your energy on constructive purposes* – If you are angry with your boss then always try to take that energy and ask yourself how you can channel it in the most positive way. Perhaps offer a powerful alternative that still achieves the objectives.

- *Prepare your staff* – Don't be fearful or defensive of your boss speaking to your own staff. Instead, coach them to get the right positive messages across.

10.3 Flatter and gain points with your boss the intelligent way

Most people dislike a "suck-up" but everyone likes receiving compliments. Studies conducted with CEOs and top US corporate managers at the Kellogg School of Management and the University of Michigan's Ross School of Business found that flattery is a successful career building technique (Stern and Westphal, 2010). Personal relationships with your boss are as important as the quality of the work you churn out. How well you have developed your personal relationship will often determine whether your work is considered an "8" or a "10" and often who gets promoted! As human beings we are never completely objective, so don't think twice. Focus on your work and building a better relationship with your boss. Here are a few tips on how to gain points with your boss without coming across as a suck-up:

- Instead of using outright compliments, frame them as questions seeking some advice. Bosses like to feel they are experts and by showing you value their opinion you are showing respect and admiration. Instead of "You did really well on that pitch to the senior managers" say "How did you manage to convince the senior managers with your pitch? They can be tough nuts to crack!"

- Don't compliment your boss to their face. Think about who their allies are in the company and tell them what you think your bosses strengths are.

- If you disagree with your boss on a topic, move on. If after reflection you feel they were right in the end, bring it up: "I thought about it and think you were right on the approach for that project." You will come across as healthily analytical but willing to concede when appropriate. No one likes someone who either agrees or disagrees all the time.

- Find out from those close to the boss what their values, opinions and social affiliations are. Surely there will be something in common with you that you can bring up, discuss and build a closer relationship on? From football to politics to bringing up your children – it all counts when trying to bond with your boss.

11. YOUR A TO B ACTION PLAN

Step 1

Review your answers and notes from the guidebook. This will include tips and ideas that you marked as resonating. Consolidate these or highlight the most important aspects in a specific color.

On the Challenge-Priority Brainstorming Chart (see Appendix) list challenges you have picked up from this guidebook, however small they may be.

Stand back from your list and see what links and connections there are – maybe use a different color to highlight challenges that have a similar source such as communication problems, bullying by boss, fear of boss, feeling inadequate in front of boss etc.

If possible, group these items under headings or concepts that you think appropriate – use your intuition and creativity here. Go as much with your feelings as your logical mind.

If you have several items for potential action, number them in priority order. There tends to be something we need to address first because it is more important to us or will give us the most benefits.

Take your top priority challenge and move on to your Thrive Action Plan (see Appendix).

Step 2

Take this top grouping/item you identified in your Challenge-Priority Brainstorming Chart.

What is the right goal or **B** here? What is going to make the most significant difference?

Try writing the goal down on a separate sheet of paper in three different ways. Which one do you find most compelling? What is it that makes it so? Think about why achieving this goal will help and what you will gain from it.

Studies have shown that people who can create a vivid image of what their achievement will look and feel like are more likely to achieve it. Take your time to really immerse yourself in this image. What you feel when you think of this image should be used as a tool to motivate yourself along your journey.

Step 3

Build on the goal to make it SMART:

Specific: As detailed and real as possible – something you can visualize clearly if you are a visual person.

Measurable: Make sure you have quantitative targets for the activity itself and the impact or outcomes you want too.

Attainable: You sense it's a stretch but you know you can do it!

Realistic: Think of the practical aspects that are necessary for success – the resources, support, strategies and tactics that will bring you success. You should be able to list these on the Thrive Action Plan, if you struggle, then your goal is possibly not realistic enough.

Timed: Build in specific deadlines – for the big steps and completion. These can be further broken down into daily or weekly goals if, for example, you need to grow your comfort zone bit by bit, day by day. Think stepping stones!

Example of a SMART boss/subordinate relationship improvement goal:

"I want to be respected and appreciated by my boss, Dean. I will begin by improving our communication and building rapport with him through our joint passion for golf. I will also look to build confidence in myself and my work through practice, support from colleagues and taking on taekwondo classes. When my relationship has improved to an amicable level I will look to occasionally ask for feedback on my work and be prepared to hear more criticism than compliments. By showing my boss I wish to improve and value his opinion and advice I will eventually gain his respect. I will assess my progress based on the feedback given by my boss and hope to improve my relationship significantly by the beginning of the new business year."

Step 4

Get going on your first action. This should be within a week from now.

Step 5

You need to get the support resources lined up.

It helps if you can inform a few well-selected individuals from your friends or family to share the goal with, seek their feedback and suggestions of how you can do things better to achieve your goal. As you move forward they can give you further valuable feedback on your progress as well as encouragement. When trying to improve your relationship with your boss you certainly don't want to be sharing this information with work colleagues. They will see you as calculating and ultimately could make your efforts known to your boss who will then see you through cynical eyes.

Think about who encourages you best, who gives you the best advice, who helps you when you are in difficulty and who may have the same developmental challenge and can go on the journey with you. Avoid sharing your goal with negative or cynical people who are likely only to discourage you.

Decide on who are the best people to help you: usually a group of 1-3 mentors.

Step 6

Decide on the frequency you are going to review your progress towards your goal – often weekly works well. What has worked well and what lessons have been learned?

Build on the successes and lessons learned and plan your next week's activities.

If you get discouraged or have a setback, don't be too hard on yourself. This can happen. After doing something that leaves you feeling positive and relaxed build on the positive momentum to press forward with your goals. Look for inspiration in this guidebook.

Be determined to take some positives out of the setback.

Ask if your goal or your sub-steps are too stretched and you need to re-calibrate or take longer. Sometimes behavioral change programs can take nine months or so!

If you really get stuck, seek help from a good mentor or coach.

Keep going.

Step 7

Success! Well done.

12. KEY POINT SUMMARY

Our relationships with our bosses can be very challenging at times, but they can also be critically important. A strong boss-employee relationship can gain us promotions, raises and open doors to new opportunities. This is without mentioning the obvious benefits of less stress and more mutual respect in the workplace.

This guidebook highlighted the importance of understanding your boss(es). This first reflection is essential in taking the next step towards looking to improve your relationship. You've had an opportunity to specifically tackle indecisive, self-centered, bullying, unappreciative and control freak bosses – frequently encountered difficult personality traits. Individuals are complex and therefore it should be no surprise that your boss may possess a few of these traits and others. Try out the recommendations made for improving communication between you and your boss. Some tips will be more successful than others. The key is to keep trying and build on what is working well. Ultimately you want to achieve an open and supportive relationship. With effort, persistence and careful observation you should get there. Good luck!

13. Useful Extra Reading

Readers of this guidebook will find great value in the *A to B Guide to Motivation* and *A to B Guide to Office Politics*. A better understanding of what motivates us and our bosses is an important first step in attempting to build a better relationship with the boss. The *A to B Guide to Motivation* also provides numerous tips on how to remain focused and motivated despite troubles you may be facing.

The *A to B Guide to Office Politics* will provide you with an overview of managing relationships with people at various levels in the organization, including your boss. If your boss plays the political card very often you'll find this guidebook of even greater use.

References and recommendations:

Brinkman, Dr. Rick, and Dr. Rick Kirschner. *Dealing with People you Can't Stand: How to Bring Out the Best in People at Their Worst.* New York: McGraw-Hill, 2002. Print.

Gabarro, John J. and John P. Kotter. "Managing Your Boss" Harvard Business Review. 01 Jan. 2005. Web. 01 Feb. 2012. <http://www.hbr.org/2005/01/managing-your-boss/ar/1>

Kanter, Rosabeth Moss. "The Cure for Horrible Bosses" Harvard Business Review. 01 Oct. 2011. Web. 01 Feb. 2012. <http://www.hbr.org/2011/10/the-cure-for-horrible-bosses/ar/1>

Patterson, Kerry, Joseph Grenny, Ron Mcmillan and Al Switzer. *Crucial Confrontations: Tools for Talking About Broken Promises, Violated Expectations, and Bad Behavior.* New York: McGraw-Hill Professional, 2004. Print.

Patterson, Kerry, Joseph Grenny, Ron Mcmillan and Al Switzer. *Crucial Conversations: Tools for Talking When Stakes Are High.* New York: McGraw-Hill Professional, 2011. Print.

Stern, Ithai, and James Westphal. 2010. Stealthy footsteps to the boardroom: Executives' backgrounds, sophisticated interpersonal influence behavior, and board appointments. Administrative Science Quarterly 55: 278–319.

Watkins, Michael. "How to Succeed With Your New Boss" Harvard Business School Working Knowledge. 03 June 2002. Web. 01 Feb. 2012. <http://hbswk.hbs.edu/item/2957.html>

ABOUT THE AUTHOR

Brian Guest is a former CEO with an extensive international career in Fortune 100 companies. Based on his experience working at various management levels and motivated by a desire to help others achieve their potential he decided to begin a career as an international executive coach.

He obtained an M.A. in Natural Sciences from the University of Cambridge, England, in 1978. Brian is also qualified as an ACA (Chartered Accountant, the UK equivalent of a CPA) in 1981.

In 1982 he began his international career on joining the American International Group (then a Fortune 100 company, the largest global insurer) as an international auditor. He was promoted to audit management and worked in the USA, Latin America, Caribbean, Europe and Africa.

In 1987 he joined Royal Insurance (now RSA) and worked in financial management in the international division.

Joining Commercial Union (now Aviva plc, 2011 Fortune Global 500 number 64) three years later, he worked in business development, holding various positions including being the General Manager for Hong Kong and Regional Director for Latin America.

In 1997 he began working in the HSBC Group (2011 Fortune Global 500 number 46) and his responsibilities over an eight year period included being CEO for the US$500mn Brazilian insurance business with 1,500 staff as well as Chief Underwriting Officer for Latin America. During this time his division received two national prizes for best performing insurer.

APPENDIX

CHALLENGE-PRIORITY BRAINSTORMING CHART

What are my challenges/problem areas?

Why are they challenges? What specific problems need to be addressed?

Can I divide my challenges/problem areas into categories?

Challenge	Priority

THRIVE ACTION PLAN

1. Challenge	What challenge am I addressing?
2. Goals	Based on my challenge, what goal can I set myself? Do I have a motivating image of the final result? Yes/No
3. SMART Goals	Use the SMART goals system to build on your goal. Specific details: How will I measure it? Time frames & deadlines: Is my goal attainable and realistic? Yes/No
4. First Step	My first step towards achieving this goal is... By when?
5. Support System	Who will be my mentors/support? What skills and resources do I have? Do I need any additional training?
6. Barriers	Possible barriers that could get in my way:
7. Review	Frequency of progress reviews & contingency plan:

ADDITIONAL NOTES

25314261R00048

Printed in Great Britain
by Amazon